Enzo Crotti

Integral 432 Hz Music

Awareness, music and meditation

WENZ BOOKS

Enzo Crotti

Integral 432 Hz Music

Awareness, music and meditation

Translation: Maddalena Rossi

Country: Italy

First Edition - August 2016

English Edition - January 2017

ISBN: 978-1-326-91982-5

"Purify yourself. Meditate. Discover the Divine.

This is your foremost duty".

(Swami Sivananda)

Dedicated to my wife Graziella
and my children Marco and Martina,
because a family in harmony
is the greatest gift one can ever receive.

Contents

Introduction

After years of writing about beneficial sound and awareness on my blog www.musica-spirito.it, I decided to use my knowledge and experience to create a new type of musical production, which I called "Integral 432 Hz Music".

This book will explore some of the concepts and theories I have been applying to my latest works, and is also designed to provide greater insight into the many facets of music as well as encourage music enthusiasts to elevate their listening experience beyond the level of mere entertainment. Though there is nothing wrong with such an approach, I have always been convinced that there is more to music than meets the eye. I also believe musicians should never ignore how their own music can affect listeners.

I have always been fascinated by what Gurdjieff called "Objective Music", i.e. a type of music that is able to convey knowledge and well-being. Pythagoras himself was said to have created music which could cure diseases.

(See. http://www.gianfrancobertagni.it/materiali/musicaemistica/

musicaogg.htm)

Nowadays, we are fairly well acquainted with the many different clinical applications of Music Therapy, so these words can sound more real, and, after reading this book, even Pythagoras will probably seem more relevant today than ever before.

My purpose is not by any means to teach how to treat diseases, but to create beneficial music and help listeners raise their awareness. I strongly believe that awareness is the key to everything and that self-improvement plays an important role in the growth of a person. That is the rationale behind my book, which I recommend reading to those who are interested in my work and wish to gain a deeper understanding of music and sound.

1

Music, a universal emotion

In ancient times music was said to be capable of arousing powerful emotions in listeners even though this view aroused controversy and was vehemently rejected by later thinkers. I am referring to the "Doctrine of the Affections", supported by some great thinkers of the past, such as Marsilio Ficino and Galileo Galilei, yet rejected by others, including Stravinsky. In his "Chronicle of my life," Stravinsky addresses the subject by saying that for him "music is, by its very nature, essentially powerless to express anything at all".

(See. https://en.wikipedia.org/wiki/Doctrine_of_the_affections)

Opponents of the Doctrine of the Affections argue that music is not inherently emotional, but it is the listeners through their cultural influences who attribute emotional qualities to it, so that someone who has never heard any music cannot produce the same emotional response as someone who has already heard and cataloged music in their brain.

However, research has shown that Ficino and Galileo were in fact right and so were especially the early Greeks (like Pythagoras himself) who laid the foundations of our civilization. A study carried out by researchers at the Max Planck Institute of Cognitive Sciences in Leipzig tried to figure out how people, who had never before heard Western music, would react emotionally when first exposed to it.

(See. http://www.focus.it/comportamento/psicologia/la-musica-e-universale)

The Mafa, an ethnic group located in the mountains of Cameroon, who had never heard any music but their own, were exposed to music by Mozart, U2, Lady Gaga etc. The outcome was very interesting, as it showed that listening to Chopin, Elton John and a lot of Western music, even for the first time, can stir the same emotions, regardless of race and culture, as if all humans were endowed with an innate capacity to understand it.

Professor Fritz, who led the research, reported that The Mafa people were able to identify the feelings expressed in the pieces that were being played. Like any Western listener, they could feel joy in speed and color (e.g. in "Are you Sleeping Brother John"), sadness in slow tempos (as in funeral marches) and distress in minor keys (e.g. in Beethoven's Fifth Symphony).

How can music affect our emotions so precisely?

In my opinion, music is capable of evoking similar emotions in different people as it is, by its very nature, similar to ourselves. Quantum physics has proven that everything in life is vibration, and the laws governing our world are very similar to sound and harmonics. In later chapters, I will try to further explain these concepts.

2

Frequencies and harmonics

What is Sound?

An acoustic wave (or sound) can be defined as a mechanical oscillation (movement in space), made by atoms and molecules through a medium, such as air, water, a wall, or anything that allows the wave to propagate. The molecules move along the waveform bumping into each other like dominoes, until they reach our ears.

Frequency refers to the number of wave cycles occurring in one second. The human ear can detect vibrations in the range of 20 to 20,000 Hz. Normally, frequencies that are higher or lower than the above range, though still existing, cannot be processed by our auditory system.

The lower the frequency the lower will be the pitch we perceive, the higher the frequency the higher the pitch.

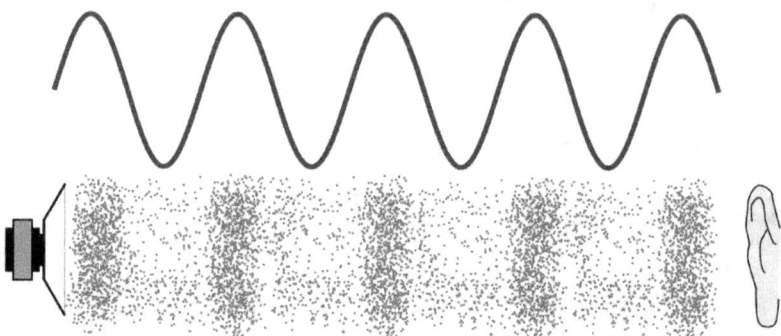

Propagation of sound wave through air.

Harmonics

Harmonics, or overtones, are a phenomenon of sound that occurs whenever sound is produced. When listening to a monophonic musical instrument (such as a flute) we might think we are hearing individual notes, in reality it is not pure notes to be produced, but rather overlapping frequencies related to each other, called partials. The lowest of them is called the fundamental, and all other resulting higher frequency tones are called "overtones". The frequency of the fundamental note has a close mathematical relationship with the frequencies of harmonics.

Given a fundamental frequency of 432 Hz (which corresponds to the note A), the first harmonic will be double this frequency (called an octave higher, that is 864 Hz) and its wavelength will be half, so it will always be an A but higher pitched than the starting A. The frequency of the second harmonic will be three times greater than the fundamental, the third will be four times this frequency, and so on.

Here are the notes we will get starting from C:

C, G, C, E, G, Bb, C, D, E, F#, G, Ab, Bb, B, C

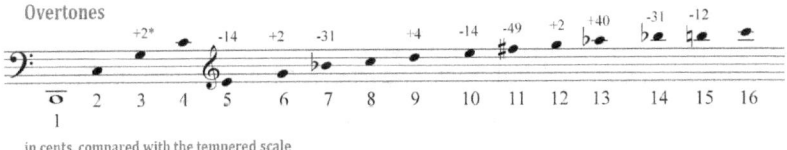

Natural harmonic series. The 7th, 11th and 14th harmonic are somewhat flat, the 13th is somewhat sharp. (Picture by Fabrizio B. at it.wikipedia - Own work, CC BY-SA 3.0, https://commons.wikimedia.org/w/index.php? curid=4909493)

The timbre of an instrument is determined by the loudness and number of the harmonics we perceive. Another interesting point is that each of the harmonics matches a specific frequency, which follows a precise mathematical relationship of the following type:

X= fundamental tone

Harmonics: X*2; X*3; X*4; X*5; X*6; X*7; X*8; etc.

The wavelength behaves exactly in the opposite way:

X= fundamental tone

Harmonics: X/2; X/3; X/4; X/5; X/6; X/7; X/8; X/9; etc.

Here's a practical example:

Supposing the X frequency of the starting fundamental tone is 256 Hz, the frequency of the first harmonic will be equal to 512 Hz (256*2), the frequency of the third harmonic will be 768 (256*3), that of the fourth harmonic 1024 (256*4) and so on, with the multiplier increasing by 1 each time.

Since wavelength and frequency of a wave are inversely proportional to each other, the wavelength has to be divided each time into a larger number. If the wavelength at 256 Hz is 1.34 m, then the first harmonic will have a length of 0,67 m (1.34/2), the second harmonic will be 0.45 m (1.34/3) and so on, with the value of the divisor increasing by one for each harmonic.

This interesting feature will be further explained later on, as it can shed some light on the relationships between sound and reality.

The Octave

The series of seven notes (1-C, 2-D, 3-E, 4-F, 5-G, 6-A, 7-B) starts over again with a C in the eighth position. This eight-note distance is called "octave" and it is a fundamental concept not only in music but in other aspects of life. As mentioned before, your starting frequency doubles with each octave, and this is a very important process to keep in mind.

In fact, as Gurdjieff explained, the octave has an esoteric significance, which underlies not only music but a lot more aspects of our world. Just think how many phenomena are based on the law of 7+1= 8: the colors, the chemical elements, the planets of the solar system, the days of the week, and many other seemingly unrelated events.

(See. http://www.ardue.org.uk/university/intro/octave.html)

3

Resonance and Entrainment

Generally, we tend to believe that what exists around us is something tangible and real, because we perceive it that way. The problem is that the word "perception" implies something that does not exist as such, but only as we experience it.

In the past, the universe was defined as something very similar to sound, as a cosmic vibration present everywhere, a sort of symphony of sound waves. I am referring to the famous idea of the "Harmony of the Spheres" put forward by some ancient philosophers, such as Pythagoras. A more recent attempt to explain the world around us is the so-called Superstring theory.

Superstring theory

According to this theory, the fundamental constituents of reality are "strings", i.e. tiny strings vibrating at different frequencies. In addition, string theory implies the existence of many more dimensions than we can perceive, as well as infinite parallel universes. It is worth noting that this quantum theory is not so different from the view of more ancient traditions (like, for example, The "Bhagavad Gita").

Everything in the existing world seems to be made up of infinitely small energy vibrations, which our senses can perceive in different modes, i.e. as light, sound, smells, etc. creating our individual picture of reality, which, by consequence, only exists within us. In fact, there are no sounds, images or smells, but we are just immersed in an ocean of frequencies.

Our brain processes the information coming from the outside, creating an image for us, but in reality nothing is as we see it. Our interface with this "virtual reality" seems to depend on DNA, or the "conscience", as others call it.

Resonance

After having ascertained that everything in the Universe is in a state of vibration, we can now talk about resonance, the phenomenon by which a body can be reached and set in vibration by another vibrating body. Such a phenomenon can be observed when a singer causes a glass to be shattered by holding a particular note long enough. Since our voice can match the vibration of the glass, it will set the glass itself into vibration. If the vibrational energy increases sufficiently the glass will eventually shatter.

Sound has therefore the ability to transfer energy in the form of vibrations from one body to another. Thanks to this quality, we can assume it is also possible to restore the correct vibration to an organ in our body that has lost its natural vibratory state, for whatever reason, and has contracted what we call "disease". Let's take music, for example, and imagine our body as a well-tuned orchestra, playing beautiful harmonious music. This would represent good health. In contrast, a musician, let's say the first violin, playing with poor timing or out of tune, would represent a sign of disease. This would almost certainly affect the entire orchestra and spoil the music altogether.

Western medicine would normally deal with such a problem by "doping", so to say, or worse by "removing" the musician. While elimination would certainly be an efficient method of solving the problem, it would also lead to an impoverishment of music. Isn't there really a less drastic solution?

Perhaps a more effective way to "correct" this failed harmonization and restore the pre-existing equilibrium could lie in making clever use of frequencies. This is exactly what happened with Shamanism and Nada Yoga, and is now being rediscovered by Music Therapy, Biopsicofonica (an Italian sound massage based treatment) and Cymatics. The principle of resonance can be used to restore balance in your life, through techniques like the healing hand, sound massage or meditating while listening to appropriate frequencies.

As mentioned previously, my purpose is not to cure any particular disease, but rather to convey an aesthetically pleasing listening experience as well as some deeper subliminal meaning through my music. My purpose is reaching a state of well-being through objective art, based on precise mathematical principles as well as on creativity. The combination of creativity and mathematics is an appropriate metaphor describing a perfect state of health, reflecting the balance between the two hemispheres of the brain, which is said to be enhanced by the practice of music.

(See. http://www.riza.it/psicologia/tu/2368/cervello-emisfero-destro-e-sinistro.html)

Entrainment

Living organisms or objects can adjust to synchronize with an external rhythm. This is the principle behind Entrainment, a phenomenon of sound where a vibrating object is made to synchronize its rate to a higher vibrating one. It follows that sound can be used to alter your brain wave frequencies, heart rate and breathing.

Brainwave Entrainment is a method which uses sound to change brain waves through specific techniques, such as Binaural Beats, Monaural Beats, Isochronic Tones, Modulations and Audio Filtering. I will not deal with such techniques in this book, but it is important to understand how sound can greatly affect brain waves and, by consequence, the mood of music listeners.

The basic brain waves are divided into four categories, based on their frequency:

- Delta Waves: 0.5 to 4 Hz, occur in deep sleep, meditation and healing state;

- Theta Waves: 4 to 8 Hz, are found in states of deep meditation, during REM sleep and in shamanic activities;

- Alpha waves: 8 to 14 Hz, are present during Non-Rem sleep or in some meditative states;

- Beta waves: from 14 to 30 Hz, dominate our normal waking state of consciousness;

- Gamma waves: from 30 to 42 hertz, are associated with extreme alertness or tension.

Music has been used for its power to induce specific brain waves since ancient times, for instance, in shamanic rituals and sacred ceremonies. The power of sound to alter brain waves and induce states of consciousness has been recently verified. These basic principles of using sound for healing and transformation can be found in every healing practice based on sound throughout history, regardless of culture and beliefs. The use of Mantra in Hinduism, Shamanism, singing and drumming in primitive cultures share the same basic use of music and sound for healing and self-transformation: Resonance and Entrainment.

4

Music Therapy and Nada Yoga

Just picture the scene and imagine that, during a concert, the orchestra, the singer or the conductor are out of sync with one another. The music would probably sound rhythmically incorrect and you would certainly request a refund for your ticket.

This is more or less what happens when the different aspects within ourselves are not in harmony and are disconnected from one another. If our body, mind and soul each work separately, in isolation, no harmony, no music can be created, but there will be only noise with no rhythm in our lives.

Picture on next page by Carlo Alberto Cazzuffi
(https://commons.wikimedia.org/wiki/File:Gaga_Symphony_Orchestra.jpeg)

As a matter of fact, we can compare man to a musical instrument, which in order to be played and produce sublime music, needs to be in harmony with itself. Our music might never be played or heard; unless we let go of resistance, it will be impossible for us to let that special music called Nada (hence Nada Yoga) vibrate inside us.

Nada Yoga, or the yoga of sound, is an Eastern discipline that uses sound, mantras and music in order to bring body, mind and soul into harmonious balance.

When we are in a state of harmony and surrender, we will be able to find unity and wholeness within ourselves. Only then will we be able to perceive, in the silence of surrender, a special music. This is Bliss, it is Nada, that blissful state of union everybody should aspire to.

Music therapy: the healing sound

Many Eastern philosophical traditions place great importance on music, for example, Mantra chanting involves uttering symbolic syllables which produce psychological and physical effects based on mathematical principles. It is hardly surprising, therefore, that music, as a form of therapy, can produce beneficial effects in patients with different types of psychological disorders, individuals with autism, for example, can greatly benefit from music within a therapeutic program led by a qualified music therapist.

Music Therapy is a paramedical discipline using sound, music and movement to produce regressive effects, to improve socialization and help individuals gradually reintegrate into the community. From a scientific point of view, Music Therapy is a branch of science studying and researching the effects of music on human cognition, emotion, and behavior, so as to find out diagnostic strategies and appropriate therapeutic procedures.

While in Nada Yoga the beneficial effects of sound, including music, have been studied and tested on normal healthy individuals for thousands of years, in Music Therapy, a Western therapeutic method, similar principles are applied to a wide range of medical conditions.

This, in my opinion, is the main difference between the Eastern and the Western approach: our culture attaches great importance only to practices specifically aimed at recovering and restoring health. That explains why Music Therapy has been around for only a few decades, while in the East the main focus has always been to make healthy people feel better, even before becoming ill, and that has been going on for thousands of years.

Ideally, we should be able to merge both cultures, so maybe we would find the true "knowledge" that still seems to be eluding us. The spiritual teacher Osho hoped that the union between West and East would provide a Superman and who knows, one day it might really happen.

(See. http://www.osho.com/it/read/featured-articles/body-dharma/the-whole-man)

Music Therapy can prove especially beneficial for some patients, as they are actively involved in the therapy through a therapeutic relationship rooted in trust and unconditional positive regard. Besides, the activities are adapted and customized each time in a mutual exchange of proposals between patient and music therapist, their reciprocal relationship being reinforced through sound. And above all, let me say, with none of the negative side effects of psychiatric medications!

Mantra and Japa Yoga

Silence, as an absence of sound, does not exist in nature, since everything in the Universe moves and vibrates. Even the farthest corners of the Universe are all movement and vibration, or matter, if you like. But we, with our limited senses, are unable to perceive it. We can only hear a limited range of frequencies and are unaware of any others coming from the Universe or even from creatures and things around us. This energy is like a subtle language which has the power to impact our lives either positively or negatively.

"In the beginning was the Word." (Gospel of John)

If you think about it, this Biblical text can be easily recognized as a sort of primordial sound. the Big Bang theory itself has led scientists to search for a particular frequency which permeates the entire Universe. In Yoga, the sound plays a critical role in the evolution of the Universe, and the initial cosmic vibration is called Nada. So silence is really not an absence, but rather a calming, comforting presence in the background.

Indian philosophy approaches this idea through the use of

Mantra, a series of sounds that help to center the mind and, through their frequencies, can also affect the human body, allowing consciousness to transcend sensory perception and connect with the cosmic vibrations.

The practice of chanting mantra is known as Japa Yoga and involves repeating one or more syllables either loudly, quietly or just mentally. To count your mantras you can use a string of prayer beads called Mala. Below are the main techniques used in Nada Yoga.

The mantra OM in Nada Yoga

A number of texts in the Vedic literature recommend meditating for a long time and in different ways by chanting the simple syllable "OM". This practice helps to get rid of impurities, according to the teaching of the masters.

Om, the most sacred Hindu Mantra.

The power of the OM Mantra resides in its symbolic value, since it allows you to tune to the original vibration of creation and, when sung on certain notes, enables to control energy through breath regulation (Prana).

Nada Yoga: The AUM mantra

In Hinduism, the AUM Mantra is the primordial sound from which the universe and all of creation first manifested, the synthesis and the essence of all mantras. The AUM embodies the energy of the divine Trinity, creating a feeling of "something that rises to the top", creating an elevating sound vibration.

In Upanishads 137-139 it is compared to a lotus, found in the center of the heart... when, chanting OM, the yogin utters the vowel A and the lotus straightens, it open when he says U; with the nasal consonant M, OM is complete... .

The vowel A helps tune into the present moment, the vowel U helps open up to other living creatures and the consonant M is for spiritual harmony.

(See. Sommovigo I. - Manuale di Yoga del Suono – casa musicale eco)

Your dominant voice tone (or ground tone)

The basic principle of Nada Yoga is that each "element" (men, animals, vegetables, minerals, molecules, atoms, etc.) has its own natural vibration.

Following this concept it follows that there is a personal sound, called "dominant voice tone" (also called "personal music", "DNA sound" or "voiceprint"), which is unique to each individual. This sound has a generally stable quality over time but can change when major transitions occur in one's life .

Special exercises help you determine the dominant tone in your voice and, by singing this note, you can find your inner harmony. This can be considered a form of "musical "meditation.

Personal voice tone is a delicate matter, because it represents the sound each person is more sensitive to, so in order to be sure to find the right one, it is better to rely on an experienced operator.

(See. http://www.musica-spirito.it/guarigione-2/tonica-personale-meditazione/)

Overtone singing

Overtone singing is a singing technique in which the singer takes advantage of the throat's resonance to bring out the harmonics present in his voice.

The harmonics are of course the ones that I have already spoken about in the chapter "Frequency and harmonics". Interestingly enough, this technique allows multiple notes to be played simultaneously by a single person. This way of singing, though varying in techniques and styles, is present in many other cultures, especially in the Far East.

Overtone singing is the top level of Nada Yoga, since it requires highly developed vocal control. The sound resulting is traditionally known as the "Anahata sound", i.e. the sound which is unstruck, according to the Hindu theory.

Practicing this type of singing helps expand the ability to listen to your inner self as well as to the world outside: this attitude will allow you to raise your awareness and achieve higher consciousness through meditation. Overtone singing can foster self-transformation, as it gradually opens and activates all our subtle energy centers called chakras, harmonizing and balancing them. So the adjective harmonic, in this case, is not only to be connected to harmonics, but also to the psychological and physical condition of the individual who practices overtone singing.

5

Awareness

Before we go any further into exploring Integral 432 Hz music, I would like to emphasize the importance of one particular topic, which I consider of fundamental importance yet is hardly ever mentioned in other spiritual books like this.

Most of the times we are not aware of what happens within ourselves, in fact, much of what we think and do happens at a subconscious level. This means we are not really in control of our own decisions and choices.

You might find this to be a little hard to take in, but for a psychologist or psychiatrist this is quite a straightforward notion. Further medical research has recently proven that in actual facts most of our decisions are made unconsciously or on "autopilot", a system ingrained in our body, which causes our decisions to be automatically generated for us about one tenth of a second before the conscious mind is even aware. It's a very fast process, but that's the way it works.

An interesting experiment:

Let's imagine a driver approaching the traffic lights. He first sees the orange light and then the red light, so he decides to brake. Logical thinking suggests that after seeing the red, the brain tells your foot to push the brake pedal. However, experimental results have contradicted this assumption.

By placing sensors on the participants' scalp to check the areas activated by the action of braking, it could be established that activation of biochemical signals did not follow the expected sequence. The area in our brain which first activates is the one transferring the impulse to brake, afterwards the visual system warns the brain that the traffic light is red. This kind of experiment was repeated for many other human activities.

This led to the conclusion that our nervous system can bypass our brain and perform the action on our behalf. When repeating a task over and over, our brain is creating a sort of fast-track for that particular type of brain impulse. So, before we are even aware of it, the impulse follows the previously repeated pattern, triggering the action.

Many of our behavior patterns are formed in early childhood and seem to be connected to the development of many of the "quirks" or even more serious disorders in adults. It is a well-known fact that the earliest years of our lives are crucially important for our development and behavior.

Living like robots

The "mechanical nature" of our behavior has been emphasized by many great masters of the past. Practicing self-awareness seems to be a great way to dramatically reduce our anxieties and worries and build self-confidence. Most of the time we go about our daily activities almost like "sleepwalkers", and this is likely to cause tension and unhappiness in our lives.

Being "mechanical" means lacking spontaneity, being stuck in the past. If our brain only works as a bio-computer, any possibility for improvisation and creativity is ruled out. This recurring pattern by which our decision-making function is by-passed, making us fall back into our habitual behavior, can be traced back to our childhood experiences. Our behavior and thought patterns can no longer meet the needs of our current life but, by now, they have become "crystallized" habits in our personality. By living this way, we get the feeling we don't really fit in anywhere. This might be fine for a creature which is hardly aware of its own existence, but for a man this is a downright tragedy. Indeed, the higher your awareness, the greatest the tragedy!

The responses we provide to circumstances in our life when we are in "standard" behavior mode are strewn with falsehoods, because they are not spontaneous. And the "deeper" we move into awareness, the more we realize this, and this often brings guilt feelings and anxiety. On the other hand, a wise person will know that there is no point in blaming oneself about it, because, as hard as things might be, they can be ultimately dealt with by adopting a new approach, which will enable us to go beyond our habitual pattern of thinking.

All we need to do is start cultivating a more focused attention to our actions, starting in small steps. While walking, you can try to focus your mind on what you are doing, instead of just letting your legs move while thinking about whatever crosses our mind. Or, every time you take a shower, try to focus on the sensations of warm water running over your body; holding your attention steady on it is already a form of meditation.

True meditation is something you can carry throughout your daily life. If you find that your mind is wandering and you are doing something else, then try to bring the two activities together by directing your focus on what you are doing. Anyone will greatly benefit from such practices, as taught by the great masters of the past, which I think are becoming increasingly relevant and important in our society. Later in this book, I will speak about "Deep Listening", as a different way of listening to music.

6

Cymatics: the study of sound waves

"Geometry is solidified music." (Pythagoras)

Sound, the origin of the whole Creation

A number of cosmological theories share the same view of reality as being based on sound with all matter being vibration. Not only that, but even man is seen as such, considering that the term person (from the Latin word "persona"), literally means: "to sound through."

(See. http://www.etymonline.com/index.php?term=person)

We have seen that quantum physics shares a similar view, but there is another Western science (or pseudo-science) which came to this conclusion long ago: it is Cymatics.

As far back as the eighteenth century, German physicist E. Chladni noted how sand placed on a metal plate could produce different geometric patterns depending on the pitch produced by a violin, thus demonstrating that sound affects matter. Those were the earliest steps in the development of Cymatics, which means "study of the waves."

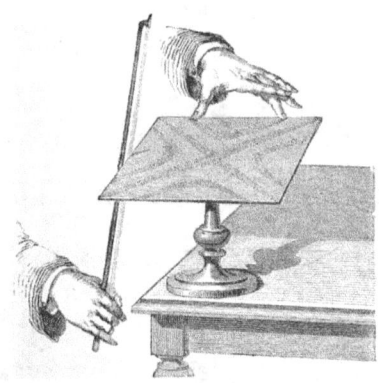

Chladni method for creating shapes with sand.

Later, Hans Jenny brought the work of Chladni into the twentieth century, by experimenting the effects of sound vibrations on various types of materials and discovering that specific sounds produce precise geometric shapes. Another fascinating finding in his research was that, by vocalizing the OM in ancient Sanskrit, the shape of the written symbol of OM appeared to form, as represented by the ancient peoples of India.

(See. https://en.wikipedia.org/wiki/Cymatics)

Equally interesting was the discovery that some of the shapes created were similar to the cellular structures of living organisms and that each cell has therefore its own vibration, in other words, its own note!

All creation is a symphony of sounds and vibrations, where individual parts are attracted by resonating with similar sounds. Those are the interesting findings of Cymatics.

Interaction between body and sound

Let us now try to understand what benefits can be derived from studying Cymatics, and hence investigate the healing aspects of music.

According to Dr. Victor Beasley-a member of a research group at the American University of the Trees, "each cell has a magnetic field which combines with the field of like and adjacent cells, thereby giving rise to the magnetic field of a particular system within the human body". The vibrations of atoms therefore create a resonance and cause cells to combine with other cells formed by similar atoms. If something within us is, for whatever reason, out of resonance, out of tune, we call it disease. Nonetheless, it will be still possible to tune our body back into harmony through meditation and music.

(See. "Nuova Era e meditazione" edito da New Sounds e "Les Nouvelles Esthétiques" Ala Editrice Milano")

Metaphorically speaking, the human body is a score, or rather a symphony, perfect as it is, that God (or Nature if you prefer) wrote for us. Whenever any wrong notes disrupted the perfection of this written score, we would need a tuner, a conductor or a guide, whatever you want to call it, to bring the whole of the orchestra back to order.

Other research has found that the human body responds to

sound frequencies even when not aware. Researcher and music educator R. Murray Schafer found that for US and Canadian students the easiest note to memorize was "B natural", while for the Europeans it was the "G sharp". This can be explained by the fact that in Canada the AC power system operates at a frequency of 60Hz (60 cycles per second), a frequency which resonates with the B note, whereas in Europe it is 50Hz, which resonates with the G# note.

It has been scientifically proven that sound can affect our body, for example, breathing, heart rate, blood pressure, muscle tension, skin temperature, internal secretion, brainwaves. Even the sounds that we cannot hear (ultrasonic waves) can profoundly affect us.

As a consequence, all the electromagnetic waves to which we are exposed can influence our body and its functions. Although music can be used as a powerful tool for restoring balance to our mind and body, it is still advisable to protect oneself against waves that are not in resonance with life, i.e. radiation emitted by power sources such as cell towers and antennae, power plants, high voltage power lines, etc. by adopting radiation shields, like those used for mobile phones.

DNA and Cymatics

Russian biophysicist and molecular biologist Pjotr Garjajev and his colleagues also explored the vibrational behavior of the DNA. Their conclusions, though maybe not well-known, were nothing short of extraordinary. They found that there is an unknown portion in our DNA which serves as a memory storage, so it does more than just building our body. Interestingly, the genetic code seems to follows the same rules as the spoken language.

(See. http://rexresearch.com/gajarev/gajarev.htm)

These experiments revealed that DNA amino-acids seem to have a syntax and semantics similar to human language, thus demonstrating that our language is not an isolated phenomenon, but is rooted in our genetic code. More important still was the discovery that it is possible to repair any sequence by using the correct resonant frequencies of DNA, avoiding the traditional technique of genetic "cut and paste". Using devices that influence cellular metabolism, through suitable light and radio frequencies, the scientists were able to reprogram cells by capturing information patterns of a particular DNA and transmitting it to another. In this way they managed to get a healthy salamander from a frog's embryo, without any of the unintended effects that can arise in traditional genetic manipulation.

(See. R. T. Tuis - 432 Hertz: La rivoluzione musicale – Nexus Edizioni)

These findings will hopefully enable us to treat certain diseases through the appropriate use of high-frequency spectrum, with the added bonus of avoiding the classic adverse side effects typically associated with drugs.

We will wait and see where this research will lead to, in the meantime we can be satisfied with these results, which, confirming once more the importance of frequencies, both on a physical and mental level, provide further evidence for the beneficial effects of music and Music Therapy on our health and well being.

Masaru Emoto and Water Crystals

Although the work of Masaru Emoto has been criticized and rejected by the scientific community in recent times, he became famous for developing a way to photograph frozen water crystals. The distinctive feature of these images is that crystal shapes vary depending on the type of music water is exposed to while crystallizing.

According to the Japanese researcher, water has the power of retaining energy, which can be triggered by sound vibrations. Some types of music create distorted shaped crystals (rock music or negative words), while other types of music make very beautiful and harmonious ones (classical music and positive affirmations).

X-ray photo of water crystal

Since our body is mostly made of water, it comes as a logical consequence that music has also an influence on us, as extensively documented by the studies on Cymatics.

To this day there is no scientific consensus on these studies, deemed inadequate and unscientific, but then, as you may know, everything today is centered on money and interests that are far removed from the beauty of Emoto's "water memory".

The world is solidified music

As we live in a world made of frequency and vibration, we can use Pythagoras' definition of geometry to define our universe as "solidified music". To gain a deeper understanding of this idea, let's begin by examining acoustic and electromagnetic waves.

In physics, an acoustic wave is explained as a mechanical oscillation (or movement in space) of atoms and molecules that travel through a medium, typically air, water, a wall, or anything that allows the wave to propagate.

So, the molecules move and fall over like dominoes, following the waveform, until reaching the human ear, yet being audible to us only if their frequency range is between 20 and 20,000 cycles per second.

Electromagnetic waves are created by the vibration of both an electric and a magnetic component oscillating perpendicular to each other and perpendicular to the direction the wave travels.

Acoustic waves are longitudinal waves that have the same direction of vibration as their direction of travel whereas electromagnetic waves are transverse waves where vibrations are perpendicular to the direction of travel, and this should be a first basic distinction in Physics. But in reality sound, like light, propagates along non-linear trajectories. The main difference between the two wave forms is that the electromagnetic wave can propagate in a vacuum, that is, it does not need matter to do so (except maybe a minimal amount), while sound waves cannot travel through a vacuum. In fact, electromagnetic waves travel at exactly the same speed as light in empty space, which is the fastest speed possible in the universe (although Einstein's theory is being challenged by recent scientific experiments at CERN in

Geneva).

Let us linger for a moment over the concept of emptiness. We know from quantum physics that what we perceive as our physical world is only a small part of reality, so there is no such thing as empty space. Vacuum is in fact "full" of a kind of matter, the so-called "dark matter" which is simply different from ordinary matter.

What does this mean? It is all about perception. If all matter is pulsing with vibrational frequencies, we can perceive something to be "real" or "dense" because of its natural vibrational state being similar to ours, in other words we perceive it this way because we share the same vibrational frequency. Hence the theories of parallel universes, as an infinite number of interpenetrating dimensions coexisting in the same space.

In view of the above considerations, we can also assume that acoustic and electromagnetic waves do not differ that much, since the only real difference between them is that the acoustic vibrations produce in us the sensation of "movement of matter" while the latter do not, otherwise they are much more similar than we think. For example, they can both transfer energy and data.

So, in the end, the ancient idea that the world is nothing but solidified music seems much less abstract than before.

7

432 Hz, History and considerations

The most acclaimed beneficial tuning

Opinions abound on 432 Hz tuning, but few studies have been published so far. In this chapter, I will try to sum up all my knowledge about it and maybe draw some useful conclusion.

Omega 432 Hz Music

The standard A = 440 Hz tuning, by which all the other notes of the scale are tuned, was adopted by the International Organization for Standardization (ISO) in 1955. The reasons behind that decision were, in my opinion, simply related to the physical properties of the existing instruments and was meant to make it easier to tune instruments in an orchestra setting (there are even some conspiracy theories accusing the Catholic Church of supporting this decision, which seems honestly quite unlikely to me).

It is a fact, however, that the current of thought called OMEGA 432 claims that the optimal tuning should be flatter than 440 Hz, namely 432 Hz. This choice would seem to have historical, harmonic and physical reasons.

Stradivari (the famous violin maker) and Verdi (the famous Italian composer) were said to compose music at 432 Hz, which was also known as Verdi's tuning, to name just a few illustrious predecessors.

(See. http://www.musica-spirito.it/musica-2/cultura-musica-2/verdi-mozart-pink-floyd-accordatura-a-432-hz/)

The most important reason for supporting this frequency lies in its greater harmony with nature and life, as also confirmed by Cymatics. It is not surprising that some sound frequencies should resonate with life and some others should not. Advocates of this frequency claim that 432 Hz is harmonious unlike the "disharmonious" 440 Hz frequency, which can cause more tension and stress than the former frequency.

432 Hz is closely connected with physiological processes of DNA and brain waves, and even with the Earth's base frequency, which is 7,83 Hz. One particularly interesting fact about 432 Hz is that, when using a natural intonation scale (Pythagorean or Just Intonation), the A (432 Hz) will appear in the same octave as C at 256 Hz, which is the fifth octave above 8 Hz, the Earth's fundamental frequency.

Andrija Puharich and 8 Hz

So, Number 8 is the reason behind the decision to tune A to 432 Hz. Number 8 is present extensively in human culture, two examples being the Law of Octaves, as taught by Gurdjieff (mentioned at the beginning of this book) and the octave in music. Moreover, 8 Hz can significantly affect our body, as discovered by Dr. Puharic.

Andrija Puharich was a pioneer doctor in the field of Electrobiology. He wrote over fifty scientific papers and patented dozens of inventions. Among other things he studied the so-called ELF (Extremely Low Frequency Waves) and demonstrated how the human brain waves are attuned to environmental ELF waves. These waves, naturally existing in the earth and occurring at an average frequency of approximately 7.83 Hz, are known as the "Schumann Resonance". According to Puharich, this frequency produces a feeling of mental and physical well-being, whereas higher or lower frequencies have negative effects on human health: 10 Hz can produce aggressive behavior, 6 Hz can cause depression. Besides, exposure to extremely high or low frequency fields can have devastating effects on our physical health, as they have high potential to cause cancer and other serious diseases.

(See. https://en.wikipedia.org/wiki/Andrija_Puharich)

In contrast, music based on multiple frequencies of 8 Hz promotes harmonization between man and nature, which is why I think we should tune our instruments to 432 Hz.

Ananda Bosman

Ananda Bosman is a musician and researcher who lives in Norway. He has carried out research and studies on the "pineal gland" (also called epiphysis) and its influence on human health. This gland is found in all individuals and is located near the center of the brain. It releases"melatonin", a hormone which seems to have anti-aging properties and plays a central role in regulating cyrcadian cycles, increasing " REM " sleep. According to Bosman, it also has a significant impact on DNA replication and therefore aging.

Activating the pineal gland helps to release serotonin, which seems to have antidepressant and immune stimulating properties.

Interestingly, the pineal gland activates when exposed to vibration of eight cycles per second (8 Hz). These vibrations may be alrcady present in the surrounding environment, which is about 7.83 Hz, the basic vibrational pulse of Earth, so that unspoilt nature makes it easier for our body to tune to this frequency or multiples of it.

(See. http://www.scienzaeconoscenza.it/articolo/8-hertz-il-codice-della-vita.php)

Music, too, can help tune to this frequency, as long as instruments are tuned properly and the harmony is based on multiples of 8 Hz, which happens, for example, when tuning A to 432 Hz.

Meditation itself, combined with the two mentioned practices, has the power to induce the so-called "Alpha" brainwaves, which help balance the two hemispheres of the brain.

Ideally, meditation should involve chanting Mantras based on notes that are multiples of 8 Hz and should be preferably done in a peaceful and harmonious place, like the mountains, or sitting on a rock by the shore, by a river and so on.

432 Hz: two different approaches

Tuning to 432 Hz can be made in two different ways. You can just tune A to 432 Hz and use the tempered scale, which is the one commonly used in the West.

The problem with this method is that the tempered scale is an artificial musical scale, designed to simplify the frequencies of the musical notes. The octave, in this way, is divided into twelve equal parts called semitones, however the frequency of C is not exactly 256 Hz as it is supposed to be, but it becomes 256.89 Hz, which does not conform to the basic principle of 432 Hz tuning.

As mentioned before, tempered tuning is an artificial one, however there are other more natural tunings, based on the natural harmonics of sound I have talked about in this book, that is the Pythagorean tuning and Just Intonation (Ptolemaic). For example, in my latest musical productions I have used a special Pythagorean tuning, which has given me excellent results, allowing me to produce 432 Hz music using multiple frequencies of 8 Hz. However, since our ear is accustomed to the tempered system, music can sound at first a bit unusual, but after listening to it again, you will start to get a feeling of relaxed ease.

Of course, tuning to 432 Hz and using a tempered scale is always a better choice than tuning to 440 Hz, so do not worry if you cannot adjust the scale on your instrument.

8

The Golden Ratio

The golden ratio, or golden section, is a mathematical representation of life and of the universe and has been an inspiration to many artists, musicians, mathematicians and philosophers throughout history. Great composers and musical bands have also used the mathematical principles underlying the golden section, so it might be worthwhile digging deeper into it.

The golden ratio is the ratio between two lines of unequal length, where the longer part divided by the smaller part is also equal to the whole length divided by the longer part. The same relationship also exists between the smaller part and the difference between the two.

This type of relationship is equal to 1.6180, known as golden number. Now, we don't want to get too bogged down in long and tedious mathematical calculations, but it is certain that the golden ratio, studied by great thinkers of the past, appears everywhere in nature as well as in architecture and the Arts. In Ancient Egypt, Ancient Greece and India, buildings, including pyramids and temples, were designed using golden ratio proportions. Later on, during the Renaissance, Leonardo Pisano (known as Fibonacci) created the famous sequence, bearing his name, of numbers related to the "golden ratio" (in which each number is the sum of the previous two: 1, 2, 3, 5, 8, 13, 21, etc.). Even Leonardo da Vinci incorporated golden section proportions into his works, especially in his famous drawing "Vitruvian Man".

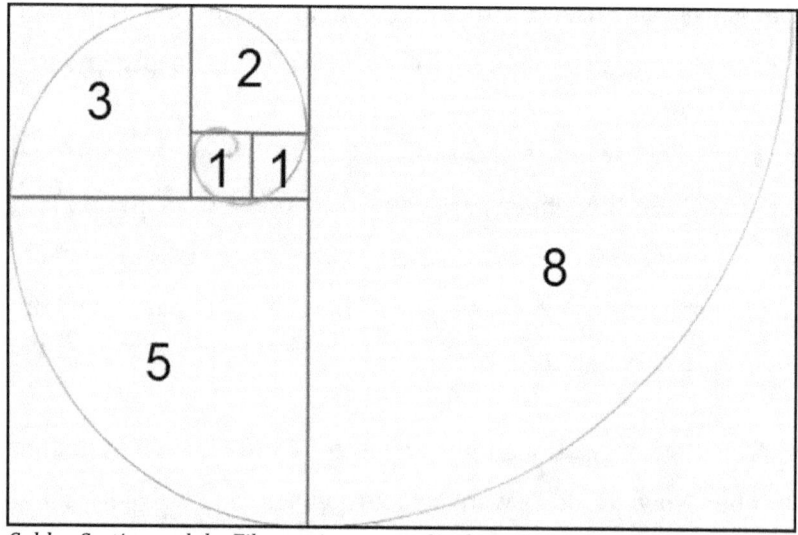

Golden Section and the Fibonacci sequence (Author: Bartolini Valerio -
https://commons.wikimedia.org/wiki/File:AureaFibonacci.jpg)

In music these proportions can be found in Bach's "The Art of the Fugue", or in Mozart's sonatas, in Beethoven's "Fifth Symphony", and in the equally important "The Rite of Spring" by Stravinsky. In the eighteenth century, there was even a Society of the Musical Sciences, of which J.S. Bach and G.F. Handel were illustrious members, studying the connection between music and mathematics.

Rock music, too, especially the so-called Progressive Rock, seems to have embraced the "mystical" side of the golden section, and more specifically the Fibonacci numbers. The most typical example is Genesis' music, where Fibonacci's numbers appear in the harmonic temporal structure of many songs: "Firth of Fifth", for example, is all based on golden numbers. Besides Genesis, other rock bands have used, albeit more sporadically, the golden numbers in their songs. Among those are Deep Purple with their song "Child in Time" and Dream Theater in their album Octavarium, entirely conceived around the ratio between the number 8 to the number 5 and the consecutive terms of Fibonacci sequence.

At this point a question arises: Why were all those scientists and intellectuals so interested in studying the "Golden Ratio"? Because they were convinced that this type of proportion was the underlying principle driving the origin of life and creation, such as the motion of planets and galaxies, the shape of cells and organs, the proportions of the human body and even the structure of our sense organs. For example, the inner ear portion called the cochlea is a snail-shell like structure based on the "spiral of Archimedes", the same found in the spiral movement of galaxies, in nature, in the relationship between the notes of the Pythagorean scale and in many other natural and physical phenomena.

Those early thinkers firmly believed that art based on golden ratio must be more natural, alive with a soul of its own, so they organized their knowledge around this esoteric concept, which was passed down to us through their creative masterpieces. The Golden Section can be used not only to plan musical compositions, but also to structure the musical scale, adapting frequencies to golden ratios. Using the golden ratio in conjunction with 256 Hz C, would therefore align our musical system with the laws of nature.

The Golden Ratio in the Musical Scale

Now I would like to deal with the Fibonacci sequence and the musical scale: the first five numbers of the sequence are 1, 1, 2, 3, 5, 8. Now, if you take the natural harmonics at these positions in the scale of harmonics, together with the fundamental tone, you will get the intervals of an octave, a fifth, a major third and an octave again.

You need just some basic knowledge of music theory to realize that this is a major chord in root position with the root doubled an octave higher. This is by far the most consonant and stable chord to our ears, and I think that its perfect relationship to the Fibonacci sequence can hardly be a mere coincidence.

9

Osho, music and meditation

Osho was a philosopher, charismatic leader and one of India's most influential and famous spiritual teachers of the twentieth century. Never Born - Never Died - Only visited this planet Earth between December 11, 1931 and January 19, 1990. His teachings also encompassed music and his thoughts on the subject can be found in his book "Musica, meditazione e silenzio" (published by News Services Corporation).

No crosses, only guitars

One inspirational message in Osho's teaching lies in his view of the cross as a symbol of punishment and guilt, as opposed to the guitar, as a vehicle for music and joy. Music itself is seen as the dance of everyday life.

Everything on Earth is laughter. Everything around us is laughing, the trees, the birds, everything except man. Our sadness comes because we are clinging tightly to words, unable to enjoy moments of pure silence. In silence there is music, there is dance, there is life, there is the temple of the divine. There is no need of ideologies, all you have to do is join the universal dance. This is the only possible revolution. All the time we are foolishly listening to people whose purpose is to make us sad, because they want to break the harmony around us. In this way, they can better exploit, enslave, oppress us.

Without harmony, we are left alone and divided, hardly rebellious. The real rebellion begins with laughter. Let's start to laugh at our religious leaders, who are untrue and hypocritical. Let's laugh at the politicians who are constantly deceiving us constantly. They are just a bunch of criminals. The day when everyone will laugh in the face of those people, their power will vanish and we will bring our guitars around, instead of the crosses we are carrying now.

Every cross we are bearing should be replaced by a guitar!

(I've added the guitar myself, although the original story was about an Indian instrument, but as a guitar player myself I think guitar can fit in quite well).

(See. "Om Mani Padme Hum", Chapter 22)

Music is like water

Music produces an atmosphere in which everything can flourish. Osho links it directly to religion, stressing how religion needs music to grow and develop in man, through prayer and meditation. Any religion that denies this direct connection between spirit and music, is contrary to nature and life.

Meditation and prayer should be filled with music, our whole being should become more musical over time. By delving deeper and deeper into music, we can reach its essence and be filled with it in a kind of communion, that is why I think all religions and beliefs should include music and give it the importance it deserves in their practices and ceremonies.

In the past, however, some religions, such as Islam or the Roman Catholic Church, were strongly opposed to music, which was seen as a frivolous pleasure, the opposite of reverence for God.

In the Islamic world, however, music has been actually revitalized by a phenomenon called "Sufism". The reason why the Sufis met with strong opposition from Islamic fundamentalists is linked to their reviving music after Islam had completely banned it. They made music and dance vital components of their ceremonies, as a means to bring man closer to God, but orthodox Muslims disapproved of their practices, which they saw as a deviation from real Islam. So they tried to kill them all, but failed. Sufism is in fact the essence, the heart and soul, the flower of Islam.

Without music nothing can ever flourish! If the atmosphere is austere, if there is no harmony, it is like trying to grow a plant in the desert; it will not bloom.

Music is instead fertile ground for the seeds of our inner self to grow and flourish, we need it like life needs water.

So let's water our souls with music! Something will surely grow.

Close up of the mystic Osho Rajneesh (Author: Sangeet Duchane - https://it.wikipedia.org/wiki/File:Osho_in_the_70s.jpg)

10

Meditation

True meditation is an elusive concept and our words always seem to fall short whenever we are trying to describe it. In the East they do have words which describe more precisely its meaning, because mediation is a long-established tradition there. In the West, by contrast, words abound for technology and science, but not for spirituality.

The first three words about meditation are also available for us in the West, and we can easily understand their meaning, yet the fourth word is not translatable in Western language, simply because we are lacking that kind of experience.

Here below are the words describing the stages of meditation, in order of depth and advancement stage:

- **Concentration:** focused attention on one single object.

- **Contemplation:** development of concentration. It is a constant focus on the same experience, going deeper and deeper in order to grasp the wholeness of it.

- **Meditation:** one of the first Western thinker to speak about meditation was Marcus Aurelius, even if he did not have a deep knowledge of it. He described it as concentration and deeper contemplation. This definition has basically retained the same meaning in the Western hemisphere for nearly two thousand years, and even today it is still connected with the word meditation.

- **Dhyan:** meaning "beyond the mind" it is neither concentration nor contemplation or meditation, as those three take place within the mind. For real meditation to happen, the mind must disappear to give way, even if for a fleeting moment, to higher consciousness. The word "Dhyan" is translated in Chinese with "Ch'an" in Japanese with "Zen" and in the "Pali" language with "Jhan", all similar words which emphasize how true meditation takes place only in the absence of the mind.

11

Music and intelligence

Recent studies suggest that music plays a major role in brain development, in particular I would like to mention a study by Professor Glenn Schnellenberg, a psychologist at the University of Toronto, showing how children engaged in music courses or lessons become more intelligent than the average of their peers.

(See. http://pss.sagepub.com/content/15/8/511.short)

The research, published in Psychological Science, was presented along with numerous other studies on the effects of music in language acquisition in children. I think the results are self-explanatory, because they proved that, even though this positive effect is probably to be linked to other extracurricular activities, with music it could be ascertained with reasonable certainty.

The study involved 144 children aged 6 years, recruited through an ad in a local newspaper. The young volunteers were offered, in exchange for their participation, a free year of music or drama classes, held by qualified teachers from the local conservatory. Not all children attended lessons at the same time. The participants, in fact, were divided into four groups: two received collective music lessons (half piano, half singing), a group followed a drama course and another group, during that year, did not attend any courses (but did the following year.) At the beginning and end of the experiment, all children were administered a standardized IQ test, specially designed for children in that age group. And the end result was that little "musicians", during that year, had scored higher in the test than the other children, both the ones engaged in drama and those who had had no lessons.

Schnellenberg reported that in every child an increase in IQ was recorded, presumably due to schooling and to other experiences that had somehow stimulated their mind. But in children who had followed the music courses, this growth had been significantly higher. An equally significant effect was also observed in children, who had attended the theater, as their social skills had improved and they had become more open and less shy.

This research, along with many others, confirms the widespread idea that musical activities are very beneficial for the overall development of children. But does listening to music really boost intelligence?

The controversial "Mozart Effect"

The dispute about the so-called "Mozart Effect" comes from the fact that this phenomenon, studied by physicists Gordon Shaw and Frances Rauscher, and published in several articles in two major scientific journals, Nature and Neurological Research, has never been confirmed by any of the subsequent experiments. *(See. https://en.wikipedia.org/wiki/Mozart effect)*

The researchers came to the conclusion that listening to Mozart's music and baroque music has the power to influence the brain and studies showed how both memory and IQ could be improved, even if for short periods, not only in humans, but also in animals exposed to the same music. Later on, the whole experiment was considered unreliable as it could never be verified by any other researchers in subsequent tests. Of course, a scientific method must follow its own rules, but remember that Shaw and Rausher are not the only ones to have dealt with this matter.

In fact, the first leading researcher of the Mozart Effect was Alfred Tomatis, who, after years of study, came to the conclusion that Mozart's music had a healing effect on the human body, as a psychological "driving force" that can help overcome emotional difficulties and communication problems. Later, John Jenkins, in his studies published in the Journal of the Royal Society of Medicine in 1993, claimed that Mozart's K448 Sonata, dramatically decreased seizures recurrence in patients suffering from epilepsy.

(See. Tuis Riccardo Tiziano – 432 Hertz, La Rivoluzione Musicale – Nexus Edizioni)

Despite the numerous studies published later, confirming the beneficial effects of Mozart's music on a variety of neurological disorders, it has not yet been possible to demonstrate a direct link with short-term neural effects. This explains the widespread skepticism about the "Mozart Effect." The German Ministry of Research published a report in 2006, which analyzed more than 300 articles published on the subject of music and intelligence. Ralph Schumacher, of Humboldt University in Berlin, explains: "One or two large and careful studies have shown a small but significant effect on IQ — which can be seen over years... but even if the effect of musical training is confirmed in future studies, it is highly unlikely to make your child a genius ."

I think these words seem to typify the results on the subject, namely that long-term exposure to music (especially well written one like Mozart's and Baroque music) can have beneficial effects on IQ, but it also yields immediate effects, if not on intelligence, on our mental and physical health.

12

Deep listening

A different way to appreciate music

Inspired by the teachings of the great masters Osho and Gurdjieff, I would like to recommend a great way of listening to music, which allows to go deeper and deeper into yourself. It is a kind of game, which basically involves using your sense of hearing as an opportunity to delve into your deepest self. First you should pay attention to any sensations and "emotions" that music produces on your body and mind.

Reaching your inner self through music will require you to go back to your "roots", learn to control the enormous energy of "emotions" to your advantage, thus achieving a balance that will ultimately lead to your "center."

Of course, there are several different types of music, each for every different aspect of your inner life. But remember that music alone will not be enough. You need to be willing to change, discover your true self and learn, otherwise even listening to the best music will become pure entertainment, a pleasant intellectual activity with no other beneficial effect.

The reason why so many scientific experiments on this subject cannot produce comparable results is simply because they are not objective, as they depend entirely on personal commitment. That's also what determines success or failure of an esoteric spiritual or whatever path you might want to take.

The philosopher and mystic Georges Gurdjieff

Reinforcing the "roots"

Let us now talk about that special part of us called "roots" and about the best music to listen to for enhancing awareness.

Our connection to the Earth, as a primal instinct with deep evolutionary origins, is what we call our "roots." The vital energy which enables us to "walk alone" and survive in the world, is located in the lower part of the body: feet, legs and pelvis. If our "foundation" is out of balance, the rest will suffer and it will be impossible to build something on uneven ground.

The music which allows you to get in touch with this aspect should be strongly rhythmical. We are therefore in the realm of percussion instruments, from maracas to congas and timpani, and even piano and guitar. Just think of tribal music, or the Brazilian carnival rhythms, which makes you want to dance to the beat and move with the rhythm. This kind of music would be suitable, as well as strongly rhythmic piano music (for example, an improvisational piece by Keith Jarrett would be perfect).

If listening to rhythmical music is already part of your nature, maybe your "roots" are already well-developed, so this could be your best choice to heighten your awareness with music.

By comparing percussions to the human heart beat, the memories of your mother's heartbeat, we can understand how deep listening of drums can help us to tap into our true potential and increase our chances of survival, making us prepared to "stand on our own feet."

For deep listening focused on your "roots" try to focus on the parts of the body that are connected to the Earth and keep us grounded and stable as we journey through life. Feel the sensations that will arise from the music when your attention is focused on your feet, legs and pelvis.

African rhythms can be a great way to listen to the "roots" (Author picture: Emilio Labrador - http://www.flickr.com/photos/3059349393/3332243434/)

A key to emotions

Emotions can closely be linked to body movement, as they are typically expressed by our voice, movements and gestures, and can affect our heart rate and breathing.

They are not located in a particular point of our body, but we can associate them with each different organ where they are accumulating at any given time.

Emotions are nothing but powerful energies, which must be released one way or another. They cannot be destroyed, but only transformed, like artists do, for example, when turning them into artwork.

Our first tool for expressing emotions is our voice, as it is closely connected with our deep self represented by breathing, which is in turn directly affected by all our emotional energies. In this sense, the voice is the most direct gateway to the soul.

Colors in music can readily evoke our emotions. This purpose can be obtained by choosing particular tones, which can induce or amplify a specific mood. The keys, the scales and the harmonies chosen by the composer typically guide the listeners by stirring up specific perceptions, and this does not depend entirely on our particular culture but, as many studies have revealed, there are inherent qualities in music colors which make them universal, and therefore "perceived" by everyone in the same way (see also "Music, a universal emotion").

Melodic instruments are particularly suited for this kind of listening. The flute, the oboe, wind instruments or stringed instruments like the violin can be used to produce strong emotional reactions. Even a piano, thanks to its wide pitch and dynamic range can accomplish the same purpose, or a guitar, with its characteristic melancholy sound. In general, it will depend on the type of composition and the tones you feel more attracted to and have the power to awaken your deepest emotions.

I would suggest selecting music that suits your current mood, or even some with a lot of color variations, such as the French impressionist music (Debussy, Satie, Ravel, etc.). While listening try to free your mind from any unnecessary thoughts, just relax. Slowly go deep inside yourself by focusing on the sensations that music produces in you, without ever judging but just witnessing. Remember that anything that might come to surface will be perfectly fine, just watch it, let it out and keep sitting calmly. If you experience a surge of energy, there is not nothing wrong, your body is just turning your suppressed emotions into something else. When you feel it is the right time to end the meditation, try to free your mind from worry and just sit listening and enjoying music, then slowly come out of your practice and move your attention to the world outside.

Centering

The inner journey will make the strings of your soul resonate with the awareness of your true self. Being centered is about being able to effectively integrate all different aspects within ourselves, balancing our body, emotions and mind to the point where reality will no longer be obscured by illusory projections, but will become much more objective.

Reaching our fullness will enable us to enjoy our uniqueness and feel we are really in control of our life. The type of music I would suggest listening during this journey to your center should be well balanced in its structure, harmony and melody, as is for example classical music, Mozart's or Baroque music by Bach and Vivaldi. Of course, you can choose other music genres and composers, as long as the music you choose can fill you with a strong sense of balance and completeness.

13

Mathematics and music

We have seen so far that math and music are closely linked, from the harmonics and frequencies of sound to the Golden Ratio. We also touched upon the Law of Octaves and number eight, a number which features extensively in human culture. At this point, I wonder: is this just a coincidence or is there some key missing link in our understanding of the connection between Music and Nature?

I think it could be Time.

Time is measured in seconds, and where does a second start?

The first definition of a second is 1 / 86,400 of the average day, which is a unit of measurement related to Earth's rotation, called day.

This means that a frequency wave equal to 1 Hz, completes 86,400 vibrations per day.

Now, notice that 86,400 is divisible by 8, and is also divisible by 432, and if we consider 12 hours, that is, half the Earth's rotation time, we get 43,200/2, which equals 432 times 100.

Now we will start from 1 Hz to see what happens when we calculate the various octave harmonics by multiplying each frequency by two:

1, 2, 4, 8, 16, 32, 64, 128, 256, 512, etc.

Here we can see that the 256 Hz C harmonic is the eight octave above 1 Hz and the fifth octave above 8 Hz, so these numbers must in some way be connected to both celestial motions and human beings, as suggested by Pythagoras' concept of "macrocosm and microcosm". This is an important piece of information indeed, because it shows our life cannot be considered separated from the planet we are living in.

Tempo

So far I have been talking about the frequencies of sound, but there are other fundamental elements in a musical piece. Among these is the tempo, i.e. the execution rate, which sets the duration of all notes in the piece.

The tempo is measured in beats per minute (bpm), so that with a tempo marking of 60 bpm we will have one beat per second. At this speed quarter notes (a note for every beat bpm) will have a frequency of 1 Hz, eight notes (a note every 1/2 beat) will have frequency of 2 Hz, the sixteenth notes (4 notes every bpm) of 4 Hz and so on. So a tempo of 60 beats per minute will strengthen the harmonic frequencies of 1 Hz, 2 Hz, 4 Hz, 8 Hz, etc. up to 256 Hz.

To conclude, we can then say that Tempo can either strengthen the harmonic effect in a piece, if the notes suggest a tempo in sync with the frequencies of the harmony, or it can counter it, if the notes are not in sync with the frequencies of the music.

Zipf's law and harmonics

At this point, you will wonder how two seemingly unrelated phenomena like frequencies and the Earth's rotation can be connected. Zipf's law can explain that, because in fact harmonics permeate many aspects of our world.

The great teacher Gurdjieff claimed, in his books, that everything that happens in our world is subject to the same laws. According to Zipf's law, apparently unrelated events, such as language, web traffic, phone calls, the ingredients in cookbooks, and many others which, logically speaking, would require different skills to be performed, are in fact connected.

Let's take for example frequency words in the English language. The most common word is THE and the second is OF, so the ratio between them is 2/1, which means that the word THE will occur twice as often as the word OF. This can be verified by analyzing any book or some site with a lot of text like Wikipedia.

Well, on further searching, we will find that the third frequency word in the English language is AND, which appears

1/3 as often as the most common word, and the following words will appear 1/4, 1/5, 1/6, 1/7 as often as the word THE and so on for all remaining words occurring with ratios of 1/8, 1/9, 1/10, etc.

(See: https://en.wikipedia.org/wiki/Zipf's law)

If this results were just limited to words and their occurrence in books and websites in the English language, it would be still interesting, yet it has been observed that it holds for other languages, too, as well as for other events like: city population size, solar flares, amino acid sequences, websites traffic, last names, quotes, ingredients in cookbooks, and many more. This same pattern of relations is found in natural harmonics (see beginning of this book). Starting with a given frequency, we will find that the first harmonic will have half the same frequency, the second 1/3, then 1/4, 1/5, 1/6 and so on.

(Recommended Video: "The Zipf Mystery" - https://www.youtube.com/watch? v=fCn8zs912OE)

I find it fascinating that the same principle can be found in so many different types of events, but that's hardly surprising if we consider that everything in this world follows a set of fixed laws. Things might be a bit different, however, when infinitely smaller or larger worlds than ours are involved (e.g. star systems, galaxies and the universe or the microscopic world of molecules, atoms and Quark).

14

Integral 432 Hz Music

You might be wondering if all of 432 Hz music is the same. By now, after years of writing and dealing with it, I can say from personal experience that not all 432 Hz music is the same.

As explained above, in order to turn to 432 Hz music, you need not only to tune A to 432 Hz, but also get C at 256 Hz, which can be achieved only by using special tunings such as the Pythagorean or Just intonation. Consequently, a piece recorded at 432 Hz, using Equal Temperament (the standard temperament in Western music), will not sound the same in Pythagorean tuning, which is based on number 8 and integers starting from 1 Hz. In addition, recording a piece at 440 Hz and then converting it to 432 Hz, might not produce the same beneficial effects as recording it directly at 432 Hz.

Tempo and Tonality (Key and Tempo)

Since the Pythagorean tuning changes depending on the key, the choice of tonality itself is important, so a piece in A-flat major in 432 Hz will not be the same as a piece in C major at 432 Hz. Besides the tempo must also be taken into account, as, measured in beats per minute (bpm), it will affect the duration of all notes in the piece proportionally. Because a minute is a fraction of the solar day, which in turn is closely related to the Earth's rotation, the importance of tempo, as connected with frequencies, cannot be underestimated; after all, sound is measured in vibrations per second (see the chapter "Mathematics and music").

And don't forget composition

Today composition is somewhat neglected, maybe because we tend to think that just listening to our favorite music is beneficial enough, which might be true and has also been confirmed by numerous studies. But let's consider for a while that the Pythagorean scale was typically used in ancient Greek modal composition and had its own characteristics. What is the highest degree of artistic perfection reached by music composed with this method?

You may not know, but the highest degree of perfection in ancient polyphony was reached not as long ago as we may think, and the man who brought this ancient music style to such degree was J.S. Bach.

Such information is important for someone who, like me, is always striving to reach the highest quality in 432 Hz music. Now I will show you how I created my latest work:

The piece is the famous "Air on the G String" by Bach, recorded in Pythagorean tuning in C major, so C = 256 Hz and A = 432 Hz. The tempo is 60 bpm, the most widely used rhythmic figures in this music (crotchet and quavers) will have a rhythmic frequency of 1 Hz and 2, which generate higher harmonics up to C at 256 Hz (2 * 1 = 2, 2 * 2 = 4, 4 * 2 = 8, 8 * 2 = 16, 16 * 2 = 32, 32 = 64 * 2, 64 * 2 = 128, 128 * 2 = 256). In other words, all the major components of this work are based on the mathematics of life, of the stars and the DNA. This is what I call "Integral 432 Hz".

For meditation lovers, I will say that the frequency of 256 Hz, if given in higher harmonics up to the color spectrum, goes up to color green (the exact generated theoretical frequency is 562,949,953,421,312 Hz). So, music could be used to meditate on the fourth chakra, also referred to as the heart chakra. The best way to listen to the piece is with headphones and also with the sound from the speakers turned up, so as to let frequencies also flow through the body. Happy listening.

(Video "Air on the G String" -

https://www.youtube.com/watch?v=nE83WoYBWZI)

Synesthesia

Synesthesia is a phenomenon which involves a "crossover" between two of our senses. It is a very interesting ability, especially for artists, as it can help explain how our brain creates our experience of reality.

We are talking about "perception" as opposed to objective reality, since it is perception which shapes the way we see reality. In fact, only a small part of all the information around us is captured and becomes available for our brain, whether consciously or not.

Some people even try to deliberately develop synesthesia, so as to be able to see things in a different way. You can attain it through appropriate training or through drugs, just like some famous artists did, for example Baudelaire, Gautier, Dali and others (though I would not encourage the latter method, because of its obvious devastating side effects). Hearing colors, touching smells, or hearing colors can be quite an unusual experience.

At an even more advanced stage, you can even enter the state of mystical perceptions and multi-sensory experiences, for example, while listening to music, you can feel carried away into a stream of images of unknown people and scents of unknown origin.

Synesthesia has been pursued by a number of artists, such as Wagner, with his theory of "total art" which implies a perfect fusion of visual and auditory clements, or painters like Kandinsky and Dalí, who tried to seek a new vision of reality, free from old beliefs and conditioning.

The concept of integral Music

The main feature of Integral 432 Hz music is that it allows to incorporate all experiences of beneficial music, awareness and meditation to create one or more pieces that are part of a work. You can meditate with music through Deep Listening, receive the most natural vibrations of 432 Hz music with Pythagorean scales and with appropriate tempos, or you can use the harmonies of Raga used in Nada Yoga. In this way, each item selected to create music is fundamentally important to achieve the desired result. That is what I mean by "Integral 432 Hz Music", which is the final goal of my musical experimentation.

15

432 Hz, questions and answers

A few of my readers have posted questions about 432 Hz music on my blog Musica & Spirito (http://www.musica-spirito.it), to which I replied with an article, which I will copy below:

After years of being interested in musical frequencies and their interaction with human nature, I will try to clarify some unresolved issues concerning the theory of 432 Hz tuning.

Points to be clarified on 432 Hz

Let's go over some concepts that many of my readers have pointed out to me as somewhat unclear, or that I myself came across on some other forum.

- If tuning A to 432 Hz is based on number 8, why isn't 440hz A just as good, since is also a multiple of 8?

- If the 432 Hz tuning is based on a more natural frequency, derived from the Schumann frequency, why do we take 7.83 Hz as a reference instead of 8 Hz?

- If I tune A to 432 Hz, why don't I get 256 Hz C?

- What are Golden Ratio and Equal Temperament?

- Did Pink Floyd and many other rock bands tune to 432 Hz or did they just tune down a semitone? What is the point of tuning down a semitone?

- What is the point of tuning A to 432 Hz if we are playing a song in Ab?

Well, I think I have outlined the major doubts that surround the theory of 432 Hz tuning. Let's try to understand more, but to do so we'll have to deal with a bit of maths formulas, and I think that brushing up our Math a little bit will not hurt anyone.

Theory

First of all, let's start by saying that all the theories you will be reading in this article have not yet received any reliable scientific support and they probably never will, because no musician could ever afford to carry out this kind of experiments. But then, as my first guitar teacher used to say, a bad engineer might cause bridges to collapse and people to die, while the worst that can happen to a bad musician is people throwing tomatoes at him.

432 Hz A and 256 Hz C

The reason for tuning A to 432 Hz is to get 256 Hz C, which would therefore be a multiple of 8, equal to 32 times 8 Hz. This is because 8 is considered a key number for human culture and nature. For example the Law of the Octave, as taught by Gurdjieff, on which the musical scale is based, or the classification of chemical elements, also based on number 8. We can also add 8 Hz brainwave, a frequency range between Alpha and Theta, i.c. a state between deep relaxation, meditation and the unconscious. Clearly, 440 Hz A does not belong here as it generates a C which is not a multiple of 8. But there is another problem: even tuning A to 432 Hz we will not get 256 Hz C. Why so?

Natural Tuning

The problem lies with the Western twelve-tone equal temperament tuning system. To get a 432Hz A and a 256 Hz C, you must use a Natural or Pythagorean tuning. The reason why the scale has changed over time is that the Pythagorean scale worked well only for early music, which lacked polyphony, relied on natural harmonics and privileged the use of a fifth interval. Subsequently, with the development of more intricate types of polyphonic textures, which occurred around the time of Bach, the chromatic scale was divided as it is today, as a compromise which does not resonate with natural harmonic frequencies, but favors the consonance of thirds, the true cornerstone of tonal music. In addition, tuning C to 256 Hz and A to 432 Hz, would mean composing music only in the Greek modes, with their particular characteristics. However, since frequencies are generated by the C note, it would be impossible to play, for example, in Db.

In the tempered system, on the other hand, A tuned to 432 Hz will give C at 256.87 Hz. Here's the formula:

$$432/2^{(9/12)}= 256.87Hz$$

Here's the result you get using the Pythagorean scale:

$$432/((3^3/2^3)*(1/2))= 256\ Hz$$

In contrast, we can see below that standard 440 Hz tuning will give C at 261.62 Hz, therefore much higher than 256 Hz:

$$440/2^{(9/12)}= 261.62\ Hz$$

Schumann Resonance and mathematics

One of the main reasons for choosing to tune to 432Hz is that this frequency is naturally attuned with the Earth's own magnetic field, better known as the Schumann Resonance, which is a simplification, in that the Schumann resonance is not exactly set at 8 Hz, but actually at 7.83 Hz.

So, if we wanted to really attune to this frequency, we should not tune C to 256 Hz, but rather to: 7,83*32= 205.56 Hz

Or 7,83*33= 258.39 Hz.

I do not think it would be easy to tune an instrument exactly in that way, but it can definitely be done with some dedicated software. Notice, however, that the Schumann resonance can depend on the Earth's radius and other variables (lightning, electrical disturbances, etc.) making it unevenly distributed both spatially and temporally around the Earth.

I think we have excellent cultural and scientific evidence to support the use of frequencies based on number 8, for example, 8 hertz brain waves of deep meditation, the many instances in which the number 8 can be observed in human culture, i.e. in architecture, the periodic table, and in the no less important musical scale itself. And more important, 8 is a number related to the planets of our solar system.

In contrast, tuning to 440 Hz does not have much historical, physical and cultural background, it is just a convention that probably became established after wind instruments in particular made their appearance, as these seem to sound better when tuned a bit sharper. Stringed instruments do not seem to be affected by this issue, as a matter of fact, when orchestras were mainly formed by stringed instruments, standard pitch used to be lower.

Tuning to 432 Hz and tuning down a semitone

We might have often heard that Pink Floyd recorded the album "The Dark Side of the Moon" by tuning to 432 Hz. First of all, it depends on what version you are analyzing, as they used to change the speed during burning and digitization, so that I found some digitized versions tuned to 435 Hz, and even to 432 Hz. The original vinyl is unreliable, as it depends on the turntable calibration, so to be sure about the tuning in "the Dark Side of the Moon" you would need to listen to the original recording tapes on a device which would hopefully match the original recording equipment. So I do not feel qualified to comment on how Pink Floyd recorded their legendary album.

Other rock bands or musicians usually tune half step down

standard tuning, what does that mean?

When tuning the guitar a half step down, the frequency of A will actually correspond to G # in standard tuning:

$440/2^{(1/12)} = 415.30$ Hz

And what will C be like in this tuning? Here's the calculation:

$415,30/2^{(9/12)} = 246.94$ Hz

This frequency is quite lower than 256 Hz, at first glance, but if we calculate 256 - 8 = 248 Hz (ie 8 X 31), we will see that it is not so far from 8, especially if we tuned A to 416 Hz, which is a multiple of 8, C would get even closer, thus becoming:

$416/2^{(9/12)} = 247.35$ Hz

But now I would like to point out an important detail: if the song I'm playing is in the keys of A major or minor, the pitches of A and C will still be relevant, but if the key is F#, will the frequency of C still be important? You also need to consider that to play with a natural scale at 432 Hz, you would have to use the Greek modes with their typical sounds. A good compromise might be to tune the fundamental note of your piece so as to make sure that most of the major frequencies are multiple of 8, even if we use the tempered scale.

Tuning almost a semitone down, that is to 416 Hz, may be great for pieces in the keys of A or E, for example, which are commonly used in rock music and are more suited to the guitar sound.

A short note on Mozart

It is often said that the Mozart effect is best enhanced by listening to pieces in Ab or Eb. Given the above explanation, we can assume the reason for this is that music in these keys is more compliant with number 8, as it is equivalent to tuning down a semitone.

Conclusions (of article)

Having addressed all the issues raised by my readers, I can now write my conclusions, but first, let me make it clear that the above are nothing more than hypotheses and conjectures. However, the rule of thumb when dealing with this thing we call Art is trying things out for yourselves and see if they work for you.

1 – Let's start by saying that choosing to tune to 432 Hz means embracing the esoteric teaching of Maths based on number 8.

2 – If you really want to get the most natural musical tuning, you'll also want to use a natural scale, where all the notes have natural frequencies. It will probably sound a bit strange, because our way of composing is different from Pythagoras' time, besides our ear is trained to hear different intervals.

The Pythagorean scale is made for modal music, i.e. ancient Greek music, not for Western music with its strong inclination towards polyphony. Using the golden scale will also mean having two different semitones, diatonic and chromatic, that is, having 17 notes in the scale instead of 12. This will, therefore, require our instruments and our musical techniques to be adjusted accordingly.

3 – That said, today the only way for us to create natural 432 Hz music is to use samplers for electronic music and compose in C major or in the Greek modes, in D Dorian, E Phrygian, etc. (Or adapt all frequencies of a piece one by one, like I do).

4 – If you want to use the equal-tempered scale and still be in tune with number 8, you will have to use a tuning which allows the fundamental tone or the most important notes in your composition to be multiples of 8. It would be useless to have a 256 Hz C or a 432 Hz A if your composition is meant to be in G # major!

5 – If you are composing music for a horror film, a good idea would be not to use frequencies that are multiple of 8, and make sure all musical elements are not in tune with the mathematics found in Nature.

16

Conclusions

(of book)

At the end of this book on 432 Hz music, I would like to answer a topical question:

"Why should you choose to tune to 432 Hz?"

The main reason lies in the "natural" quality of 432 Hz frequency, because it has a direct connection with the Earth's rotation and the frequencies that surround our lives. I believe that our musical microcosm should not be separated from the surrounding macrocosm, that is the Earth, Planets, Sun and their frequencies.

After these chapters dedicated to music and awareness, I hope I have made my point clear about the purpose of my musical research and "Integral 432 Hz Music". You may still be wondering, though, why I said that the Pythagorean scale may fit ancient Greek music but not Western music.

In fact, to play with Pythagorean or Just Intonation (Ptolemaic) scales, we would need musical instruments that are different in construction from the ones we use today, and even with the notes tuned properly, there would be still limitations, preventing the execution of too sophisticated harmonies. In other words, with a single tuning you can only play in a key at a time.

Fortunately, nowadays we can rely on advanced computer technology, so that sampling programs and music editing make it possible to change tuning even to songs that were not created using natural tuning. The process is quite complicated, as it involves manually adjusting every single note of a song, and believe me, there are plenty of them in a piece like "Air on the G String"!

In any case, with a little patience (and a lot of work) you can get a full natural 432 Hz tuning, at the right tempo, as if all instruments had been properly tuned right from the start.

Well, we'll see where my research will take me, in the meantime, I hope this book will open up new possibilities for you and your music that maybe you did not think of. Before leaving, I would like to invite you, if you have not already done so, to visit my website and listen to my music. Namasté.

Essential Bibliography

Enzo Crotti – Nada Yoga, Musicoterapia Orientale – digital ebook

Goldman Johnatan – Healing Sounds: The Power of Harmonics – Healing Arts Pr

George I. Gurdjieff – Beelzebub's Tales to His Grandson: All And Everything: 1st Series (Compass) – Penguin Books

Osho – Musica, Meditazione e Silenzio - Oshoba

Derrick Scott Van Heerden – Mathemagical Music Production – digital ebook

Sommovigo Ida – Manuale di Yoga del Suono – Casa

Musicale Eco

Tuis Riccardo Tiziano – 432 Hertz, La Rivoluzione Musicale

– Nexus Edizioni

Luca Vignali – L'Arte di guarire con la musica – Edizioni il

Punto d'Incontro

Essential Websites

www.amadeux.net

https://it.wikipedia.org/

www.lorecalle.it

www.meditare.it

www.musica-spirito.it

www.nadayoga.it

www.osho.com

http://rexresearch.com/

http://www.scienzaeconoscenza.it/

The Author

"Purify. Meditate. Discover the divine. This is your highest duty." (Swami Sivananda)

Namasté, my name is Enzo Crotti and I am a guitarist, composer and researcher. My mission has always been to promote knowledge through my work, by combining both aesthetic and beneficial aspects of music, which ultimately is  what I think real art should be about.

For years now I have been writing a blog about music and the profound effects it can have on both human mind and body. I hope my work will be useful to you and I thank you for taking the time to read my words. Do not forget to check out my site. Thank you.

Enzo Crotti

Web site: www.enzocrotti.com